The Confident You

6 strategies to claim your personal power
for abundant living

JANA CORINNE

JANA CORINNE

ISBN: 9781096426769

DEDICATION

To my daughter Madison, you are my greatest joy in life. May you know what it is to live life to the fullest and create the life you desire.

CONTENTS

ACKNOWLEDGMENTS

I am no English major and writing a book was more difficult than I had imagined. Thank you to my editor, Deana Scruggs Vanderaarde who helped me to get my thoughts organized on paper. Thank you Deana for your insights, encouragement and support. To my husband Tyler, you are my rock and my comfort. Thank you for supporting our family while I chased my dreams of entrepreneurship. To my mother Mary, who encouraged me to write this book and was my first example of how hard work and believing in yourself leads you to success. To Amrit, Dede and Sarah, who continue to teach me the value of loving friendship. And to my dad, David, who always made me feel like I was the important thing in his life and who pushed me to higher achievement.

"To live is the rarest thing in the world. Most people exist, that is all."

—Oscar Wilde

1 BREAKING THE CYCLE

We all have dreams—dreams of a fulfilling career, loving relationships, a healthier body, personal achievement, and many other life enriching experiences. It's important to allow ourselves to dream. All of the wonderful things we enjoy in our lives were once someone's dream—that house you live in, your favorite restaurant, the car you drive, the company you work with, the shoes on your feet and so on and so forth. When we allow ourselves to dream, we open up ourselves to so many possibilities.

If you have been struggling to achieve your dreams, you may be experiencing an array of emotions such as frustration, anger, sadness, loneliness, doubt, worry, discouragement, etc. Quite frequently, we tend to bounce between the emotions of sadness and anger in a "crazy eight cycle"—a term coined by Life Success Coach, Anthony Robbins. Human beings need to feel significant and connected. When things don't go our way, and we feel powerless to change them, we tend to become angry because the physiological state of anger feels powerful.

Think about how your body feels when you are angry—every muscle in your body is tense, you are pumping adrenaline and you feel like you could really kick someone's a**. You can only sustain this intense state for so long until you become tired and your body needs to rest. You may then slip into sadness or label yourself as "depressed". The phrase "I'm just so depressed" gets thrown around a lot in our culture—some may use it to describe feeling sad.

When you are in a state of sadness, your body rests and you connect with yourself. Anger makes you feel significant and sadness makes you feel connected. I have been caught in this cycle many times (it's exhausting!) and found that the best way to get yourself out of the cycle is to do these two things:

> 1) Meet your need for significance and connection in a way that is healthy and good for you. The best way to do this is to shift the focus from yourself and your "problem" and give to someone else. In serving others, in giving of your time and energy, you play a significant role in their lives AND it allows you to connect with another human being. Not to mention it really puts life in perspective for you!

> 2) Let go. Let go of the worry and let go of your tight grip on the "problem". Trust that the universe will bring to you what you ask of it.

I have witnessed others caught in this "crazy eight" pattern and I can tell you it's not a pretty sight. In listening to them speak about the struggle to achieve their dream, you can really feel their anger and resentment. You can sense the defensive, fearful and downright negative vibe ~ which ironically closes them off from new opportunities.

Further, when we allow ourselves to stay in states of sadness, we become discouraged and slip into an "impossibility mentality". We use language like "can't" and "never" in our self-talk. This constant, negative self-talk further leads us to believe that we cannot and will not experience our dream come true. We creatively imagine many reasons why we cannot attain our goals and seek out evidence from others in similar situations to confirm these beliefs, which further affirms our choice to give up.

We may also look at others who have successfully achieved their goals and justify our own situation by pointing out the differences between us and the happily successful person. The fatal flaw here is that the language we use to speak to ourselves (the language of our inner voice) has now set our way of thinking to "impossible", rather than possible.

Ever heard of the "self-fulfilling prophecy"? The term "self-fulfilling prophecy" (SFP) was coined in 1948 by Robert Merton to describe "a false definition of the situation evoking a new behavior which makes the originally false conception come true".

Our thoughts influence our behaviors and our behaviors influence our actions and our actions produce the results in our lives.

Thought—>Behavior—>Action—>Result

The good news is that thoughts are within your control! You can be surrounded by others in a crowded room and yet still think you are lonely. You can be alone in the Alaskan wilderness, the nearest human being five miles away and be completely happy. No one can make you think anything but you.

At best, others can trigger you or influence you to think a certain way, and yet what to think and what not to think is ultimately your decision. Being without your goal can trigger feelings of scarcity, but you do not have to stay in scarcity mode. You can change your mental state in a matter of seconds by changing your thoughts. You can choose to have an "impossibility mentality" or you can choose to speak to yourself in a way that creates opportunities.

For those of you who are feeling that your hope of realizing your dream is dwindling, know that the universe has something special for you, no matter your age, situation or circumstances. You just have to trust yourself! It may take a little longer than you planned, but remember: the universe is on your side!

When we say 'try', we tend to set ourselves up for failure because we are including the possibility that it may not happen. Removing the 'try' word from our mindsets does wonders for us! Make the decision to 'do' something, instead of 'try'.

Whether you have recently decided to open yourself to finding a companion, starting a new business, making a career change, being healthy, or another goal, no doubt at some point the following questions have crossed your mind:

When will it happen for me?

Where will I meet the one?

How will I start my own business?

When should I get into this new career?

Will I know? Will I be ready?

I believe that people come in and out of our lives at specific time periods for a reason. I believe that we are brought together and connected with each other to learn life lessons and to grow. No doubt you have learned various lessons from your past relationships and experiences and have grown in many ways. The key now is to learn and move forward. The caution is not to allow past failures and fear to hinder you from new opportunities to create a new life for yourself.

When we fail, there is a natural grieving period and this period is different for everyone. However, sometimes a person fails to move out of their grief and becomes stuck in the memory of the past.

We mull over what went wrong: how we could have avoided it, what we 'should have done', why it happened. We analyze it over and over and over in our minds. We tell the story to those in our close circle, connecting with others for insight and support. They often give us sympathy, advice and validation.... those wonderful things that friends and loved ones do for each other. We all need someone we can talk with, express ourselves to—a shoulder to lean on (and sometimes to cry on).

Unfortunately, we often get so caught up dwelling on a past failure that we miss new opportunities for love and life. Why do we dwell? For some, we feel that we have "unfinished business"—that we did not get the closure we need. The common quick fix is to overanalyze the past failure in an attempt to gain closure—but that is not necessary. When we choose this route, we are sucked back into the past and experience the hurt all over again, putting us back in a frame of mind which further inhibits us from moving forward.

We may become so focused on what is behind us that we cannot live in the present or look forward to the future. Our mindset can become clouded with fear of repeating the same negative experiences. This fear keeps us from being open-minded and thinking clearly about what we want. When we operate from a place of fear, our focus tends to be on what we DON'T want rather than what we DO want.

Have you ever heard the phrase, "You will either be motivated by a dream or a nightmare"? This describes the difference between people who seek to AVOID something and those who seek to GAIN something. Harmless, right? But remember: your focus will be your result.

According to Neuro Linguistic Programming (NLP), our subconscious cannot distinguish negative directives. I'll give you an example:

Do not think about yellow flowers.

What just happened? For a split second a visual of yellow flowers flashed in your mind before your conscious mind pushed them away.

Your subconscious doesn't understand that you are using the word 'not'~ neither does the Universe. In dating, have you ever said to yourself, "I don't want a _____ man/woman", and noticed you seem to attract exactly what you are trying to avoid? Your subconscious influences you to behave in ways that attract the very thing that you focus on: The Universe grants your wish.

The moral of the story? Focus on what you DO want.

A lack of mindfulness, of not being intentional, can keep us from opportunities for a new future. When we dwell in the past for too long we self-sabotage our opportunities in the present.

Our continuous focus on the past keeps us there—we REPEAT the behaviors of our past self and therefore continue to get the SAME results. A younger version of ourselves is running the show, so to speak. We all are familiar with the definition of insanity. Instead, make the CHOICE to no longer dwell in the pain of the past ~ that it no longer has a hold on you.

Previous experiences often lead us to operate from a place of fear and scarcity. If we have been burned in the past, we will do almost anything to protect ourselves from being hurt again. We know that opening our heart means being vulnerable to the possibility of pain. We are reluctant because the memory of pain is strongly engraved in our subconscious and conscious minds. We have formed beliefs from past negative experiences and our subconscious influences us because of those beliefs. This fear and scarcity holds us back from opportunities to meet and connect with others. Often, new acquaintances don't truly get to see the wonderful person hidden behind the protective wall of fear, thus the connection never takes place.

"You may be hurt if you love too much, but you will live in misery if you love too little." — Napoleon Hill

A victim mentality (low self-esteem and poor self-image) influences our behaviors and actions. The effects from a past abusive relationship can keep us from attracting the right people and opportunities to us. When we have low self-esteem and a poor self-image, our true self cannot shine through. The universal law of attraction states that like attracts like and so negative energy attracts negative energy.

This was me for quite some time. My victim mentality, low self-esteem and poor self-image continued to attract insecure, controlling types of people—in my workplace, social circle and love life. I quickly slipped into victim blaming and victim shaming; often wondering, "What's wrong with me? Or "What am I doing wrong?".

When you are caught in a victim mentality, it is quite common to think that the universe is against you. It seems that every step you take leads into one undesirable situation after another and you cannot find a way out of this endless maze of frustration and disappointment.

If you continue in this mentality, you can develop the very dangerous false belief that EVERYTHING in your life is outside of your control and you are powerless—like a rowboat without oars, drifting on the ocean, taking a hit with each massive wave. The danger is that your perspective changes, you no longer feel you have any personal power, therefore you can't use it to affect your desired outcomes.

Settling for someone we are not truly interested in is a common action when we are afraid of being alone. Staying in a job we hate because we don't think we can find a better one gives us a false sense of security. Under cutting your prices just to attain a potential client's business feeds our sense of scarcity —*that we and what we offer is not enough.* I have experienced this mentality and it certainly creeps up on you! This FEAR leads to settling. Settling leads to disappointment and ironically, more negative feelings!

It is fear that makes us settle. We are just comfortable enough to get through another day, week, year. *Not good enough to stay, but not bad enough to leave.*

Fear of rejection may play a large part in hindering our search. We have opportunities to meet new people but are afraid to walk across a room to introduce ourselves or send a message to someone. We fear judgement or rejection which will cause embarrassment and be a low blow to our self-esteem ~ to protect our self-esteem, we take no action. Ironically when we realize we still don't have what we want, our self-esteem suffers further.

It can seem daunting to put yourself out there when you feel you are not ready. It is common to feel too shy to meet new people outside of your social circle, to go to that interview, to meet with your first customer or client. Maybe you feel as if you need to lose X amount of weight, or buy a new wardrobe, or get another degree, etc. It might be the feeling of mental and emotional exhaustion ~ you may feel that you just don't have the energy to start a new venture.

Our inner dialogue invents all sorts of reasons that we cannot achieve our goals:

I am 'too old' or 'too out of shape'

I don't have many options

I'm not 'tech savvy' enough

I'm afraid to be judged or rejected

I'm afraid of attracting the wrong type of attention

I attract the unemotionally available or player types

I'm always placed in the friend zone

I have no idea what I'm doing

I'm not smart enough

I'm not the 'right type' for this sort of thing

I'm not wealthy enough

I just cannot take another unhealthy relationship

I feel I have 'too much baggage'

I'm 'unapproachable' or 'too intimidating' to ask out

I'm not _____ enough

Most of us have an extensive list of reasons, or tasks we need to accomplish, before we can even 'put ourselves out there' or begin taking action, so we delay starting. We don't reach out to meet new people, we don't get out and socialize, we don't create the website, we don't start conversations, we don't advertise. I call this 'getting ready to get ready'. The truth is, when we wait to 'get ourselves ready', we close ourselves off from opportunity.

What have you been avoiding lately? What excuses have you been making that have stopped you from progressing forward? How long have you been stuck?

The fact that you are reading this book tells me one thing— that you are ready to make a change. You are done avoiding your problems. You are fed up with going through the motions. You want more.

You know deep down that there is a better life for you—and YOU are the one who is going to create it my friend!

Through the next several chapters, think of me as your personal confidence coach. I want you to realize the power you have within you and put it to good use. I want you to see yourself clearly for the first time in a long time, or maybe ever! Come along with me on this journey to the new confident you! Are you ready?

2 SIX STRATEGIES TO CREATE THE CONFIDENT YOU

You have the power to attract and create your dream!

This power is in your personal transformation of manifestation, energy, and action. Two very important parts of this transformation are: developing a mindset that enables you to operate from a place of self-love, true confidence, abundance, and believing that there is a higher intent for the relationships you form with the people who come in and out of your life. It consists of six strategies to set you on the right path towards achieving your goals. I gathered these strategies from various sources of inspiration:

1) My own personal journey: from a place of low self-esteem, loneliness and despair after having been a victim of abusive relationships to a place of true self confidence and vibrant energy, allowing me to attract the right people into my life and create a loving, happy marriage and a wonderful business that fulfills me.

2) Approaches from my coaching practice that I use when guiding clients to achieve success in creating true confidence, love, success and happiness in their lives.

3) My studies in various forms of psychology and my strategic intervention coach training.

In this book, we discuss the methods whereby you create the mindset needed to achieve your goal. We also discuss the actions, the steps you can take to attract and create the life you want. Once you harness the power of these strategies, you will be able to attract the right people (whether it be friends, partners, lovers, customers, clients etc) to you and stop wasting your time and energy on those that are not a good fit for you.

I have learned that if you are unhappy with an aspect of your life and you want to create a change, you begin with a change in your mindset:

Thought—Behavior—Action—Result

Your thoughts influence your behaviors ~ your behaviors influence your actions ~ your actions produce the results in your life. If you want to change the results in your life, start changing the way you think.

Mindset work is important for any goal you want to achieve. Successful people know this well. Developing a daily mindset practice is a common characteristic of those who have achieved their greatest goals. A wonderful example is the famous athlete, Mohammad Ali. Every day, the young fighter thought about being the greatest, behaved as if he were the greatest, trained as if he were the greatest, until one day he in fact was the greatest!

Physiology also plays a key role in changing the way you think and feel. Many mental health professionals use the term 'body-mind' to describe the mind and body working together as an integrated whole. I won't go into extensive detail, but it is important for you to understand that at the neurotransmitter level, there is no separation between the body and the mind. What does this mean for us? It means you can also shift your mindset by changing your physiology. Go ahead and try it!

When you smile you instantly feel happier. When you stand up straight and tall with your shoulders back, you immediately feel stronger and more confident.

Your body and mind are connected. Use this knowledge to your advantage ~ know that you can get yourself into a positive mindset whenever you want, wherever you are.

Those who have achieved any substantial positive health change or weight loss have done their mindset work. Those who have achieved greatness in their career know its importance.

Those who have found their life-long partner and created a successful marriage, know the value of formulating their mindset to be confident, open to love, inviting love, and upholding the highest intentions for the relationship at all times.

You now know that mindset is very important for attracting and creating the life you desire, but it is not the only piece of the puzzle. You must also take ACTION! The action sequence is our bridge to the end result. One can easily get hung up in the thinking and talking stage, and miss transitioning into the action stage. We all know that it is one thing to 'talk the talk' yet quite another to 'walk the walk'! This is why positive affirmations alone do not produce the changes you seek in your life.

Many years ago, I was caught in an abusive romantic relationship, with few options to get out and unable to leave without risking my safety. Once I made the final decision to leave and sought help from some wonderful friends, I left the situation. Yet as I began dating again, I continued to attract the same type of partner and seemed to be repeating the same pattern! The same was happening in my career. Around the same time I left this bad relationship, I left my job. A few short weeks into my new job and I realized I was in a similar negative situation with verbal and emotional abuse, bullying, and various other issues. Different partner, different company—same situation.

It wasn't until I began my personal transformation that my life really started to change for the better.

By using the strategies I am about to share with you, I was able to transformation myself from insecure, lonely, and sad to confident, strong, and happy! This allowed me to attract the right partner for me and create a loving and fulfilling relationship with a man who would later become my wonderful husband. This allowed me start my own businesses and fully utilize my talents and choose who I wanted to work with.

These methods helped a warm, charismatic and humorous woman who was struggling to move forward from the pain of an abusive marriage. It was difficult for her to be vulnerable and trust any man because of the past mental and emotional abuse she had endured for so many years. Through her personal transformation, she found the strength and confidence to begin dating again and met a wonderful, warm and humorous man to whom she has now been happily married for 5 years!

Another highly educated and ambitious women saw her dream business become a reality. She struggled to leave her job, as she had been there for almost 20 years. She was afraid to leave the "security" of her paycheck but could not sit another year at her desk unchallenged, dreaming about the business she wanted to create and watching as the months went by on her desk calendar. She took the first step into transitioning into entrepreneurship, growing her business, until the day came she was able to fully step away from her job and give her full energy towards expanding her impact globally on women in need.

Another kind-hearted and intelligent woman completely changed her dating life. She had repeatedly attracted men who did not return her love and respect. She found herself either being placed in the friend zone, used solely for a casual sexual relationship, or as a 'stand in girlfriend' until the guy felt that something better came along. When she went through her transformation she began to focus on her needs and wants, quickly recognizing and disqualifying those types of men, choosing instead to spend her time only with the ones who truly respected her and valued her company ~ and who she actually liked!

An easy-going and hardworking man who found himself being used solely for his income and status, decided 'no more!' and started his transformation. He began by setting his own standards, learned how to protect himself from 'energy vampires' (money is a form of energy), and began respecting his time by setting boundaries. He went from dating women who were secretly married, looking for a sugar daddy boyfriend, to dating a genuine woman who truly shares his interests and cares for him deeply. He is now happier and so much more fulfilled!

Another client who benefitted from these strategies is a gentle, nurturing, gorgeous woman who was extremely talented and skilled at helping others become better managers and leaders. She struggled with her own confidence to expand and reach a larger clientele. She was afraid to "put herself out there". She is now doing Facebook Live, authoring her own books and traveling globally to teach and coach others on leadership.

These methods have enabled many men and women to find their personal power and create the life they desire. My hope is that you will utilize them to do the same!

Now that we have touched on the benefits of these strategies, let's dive right in and get started!

3 STRATEGY #1 MAKE YOUR MIND WORK FOR YOU NOT AGAINST YOU

How do I attract the right opportunity for me? How do I stand out from the millions of other fish in the sea? How can I be found among all the noise, alerts, technology distractions—the hustle and bustle of life?

Life is so busy these days: With 'to-do lists', social obligations, work, business, errands, and chores, who has time to focus on personal goals? Who has time to meet? Where do I find opportunities? A random run-in at the gym? Walking my dog at the park? At a conference? Through my matchmaking friend who is trying to hook me up with her neighbor?

It looks so easy in the movies! You bump carts in line with a new friend at the checkout, strike up a conversation and exchange numbers. You just happen to run into an old colleague walking down the street and they just switched companies and have a new position you might be interested in, or you end up sitting next to your next business partner on a bar stool exchanging witty banter. But how will this happen in my life? How do I find my next idea? How do I approach someone and ask for their business without seeming desperate? Or too pushy? So many variables go into finding your next opportunity it can feel quite overwhelming.

Making THE Decision

The search for opportunity can often seem daunting, frustrating, or nearly impossible. We become discouraged if things don't happen for us right away. Regardless of the struggles and frustrations you have encountered in the past, it is up to you to make your decision.

The decision is whether you WILL or WILL NOT have the life you desire. This decision needs to be based on a purpose.

What is your purpose for having a romantic, intimate relationship? A fulfilling career? A successful business? A healthy mind and body? Another way of thinking about it is to ask yourself: What is my 'WHY' factor? Your 'WHY factor' is what gets you through the challenges: both external and internal.

No doubt love, happiness, and wealth come to mind, but I encourage you to give yourself time to dig deeply for more answers. When we explore through writing, it is often the answers near the bottom of our list that reveal our core values. Give yourself the time to spend on this exercise.

Set a timer for 20 minutes and ask yourself the following questions, writing down your answers:

What do I really want?

Why do I want this for myself?

What will this relationship/job/business/healthy body do for me?

How will having this _____ change my life?

How will having a _____ change me mentally? Emotionally? Physically? Spiritually?

Please take a moment to reflect on your purpose for your decision.

Once you make the decision that having your dream is truly what you want, shift your mindset toward success and your desire is communicated to the universe.

Pay attention to your language...

Instead of 'Maybe I'll find someone for me', (possibility in the future tense) or

'I wish I could find the right job for me' (wishing it were possible) or

'My goal is to one day own a successful business' (stating a future goal), reframe your thought to be:

"I am a successful business owner".

"I am living the career that I want".

"I am with the person who is right for me".

Shift to the present tense. Sit up straight, close your eyes and say it out loud with assertion.

Choose your words to explain not a distant hope or wish for the future, but a process that is occurring right now. Treat it as if it is already happening. See it, hear it, feel it, taste it as if it were already happening right now. Your subconscious will start working for you to make it happen!

Rewriting your storyline by updating your roadmap

We all have preconceived notions about ourselves, other people, and our environment. As human beings, we use our five senses to take in information, process it, and assign it meaning. When we give value to our experiences we store this information and it becomes part of our belief system. Beliefs, stereotypes, and fears are formed for a reason ~ they are the way we protect ourselves and navigate our world.

According to Neuro-Linguistic Programming, from birth to age seven we are in the imprint period, most of our learning is from our parents and is unintentional on our part.

From ages eight to thirteen, we grow into the modeling period where we both consciously and unconsciously learn from copying friends. During this phase, important core values are formed. We then enter the socialization period, ages fourteen to twenty-one. In this stage of our lives, we assimilate beliefs that affect our relationships.

We seek to strengthen our beliefs through evidence from our environment ~ we look for information that confirms our beliefs and tend to ignore that which doesn't. Our conscious brain is trying to make sense of things and to connect the dots. The mind is a powerful processor.

As we go through life, we continue to make decisions based upon our beliefs. Our belief system becomes a road map, guiding us in our journey through life.

But what happens when we begin to grow out of our small world? What happens when we venture out into new worlds? New environments? New people? New challenges?

We are forced to change and grow.... we learn new things! Many of our beliefs are challenged: sometimes our perceptions change and we start to think differently.

We need a fresh roadmap to navigate unfamiliar terrain.

What happens if you are using an outdated road map, a map that is no longer relevant in your present journey? People relying on an obsolete roadmap feel lost, confused, tired, frustrated ~ as if they are going in circles, never arriving at their destination.

They may have trouble forming relationships with others, repeat the same negative patterns in different aspects of their lives, or attract the same people and situations towards them. Does that sound like fun to you? No!

No one likes to be lost in the jungle, scurrying around in circles, straying from their path.

You want to be driving on the right road to take you to the beautiful island just over the bridge!

So how do you know if your road map is outdated?

- You see others who are attracting and enjoying great relationships, careers, health, etc and you wonder why you can't do the same

- You know you're a valuable person with gifts, talents, and personality but have trouble convincing others that you are

- It seems as if you're spinning your wheels and getting nowhere. You may feel lost, confused, frustrated, wishing you could 'find the right path'

- Positive affirmations and positive thinking don't produce results for you (I'll explain why later)

- You have trouble attracting healthy and happy relationships

- You find yourself constantly placed in the 'friend zone'

- You attract the 'unable to commit' or 'emotionally unavailable'

- You continue to attract the manipulative, abusive, or controlling types in social circles, clientele or the workplace

- You self-sabotage a good relationship before it has a chance to grow further

- Your self-image is poor, negative, or out of alignment with your ideal self

- Your circle of friends consists of people who constantly complain, sap your energy, waste your time, and inhibit your growth

- Your personal health is suffering~ you feel tired, dull, sluggish, moody, and negative

If you're following an outdated road map, it's time to upgrade to a new, highly advanced, highly accurate, GPS system! By updating your navigation system, you'll go from feeling lost to confidently driving toward your destination.

There are different methods of achieving this: meditation, self-hypnosis, or through mindset exercises. I encourage you to find a practice that best suits you. The goal is to get rid of the self-sabotaging beliefs that have been guiding you and replace them with new ones that better serve you.

If you need assistance finding a practice that works for you visit www.janacorinne.com and reach out to me.

Now I will show you a mindset exercise you can implement immediately:

Achieving Total Clarity

What do you want? This is the first question I ask my clients in our first session together. It seems such a simple question. But you would be surprised how many people don't truly know what they want. Either they haven't taken the time to dig down deep into their heart's desire, or they are afraid to ask for what they truly want for fear of disappointment or shame. Sometimes what they think they want is really someone else's dream. It could be the dream of a parent, a spouse, or an authoritative person in their lives. This question ALWAYS takes some time to answer. We burrow further and further beneath their surface words into multiple layers of meaning, where we find their heart's true desire! So, let me ask you a very important question:

What do you want?

Create a list of all the characteristics of your ideal relationship/career/business/health/social life, etc. If you need some structure, you can break your characteristics down into 4 categories:

Physical
Mental
Emotional
Spiritual

Really spend some time on this part. Set aside a block of time for yourself and turn off all phones, alarms, or anything that will distract you. This is your time to daydream about what you want. Hold nothing back!
Do not let your mind wander into '*how* will I find this?' or '*where* would it be?' or "what *should* it be?". Don't worry about the HOW, focus only on your WANTS.

If you let fear or doubt creep into your mind, your list will not be the full representation of what you want, but rather a list based upon dread and negative beliefs that will not serve you. If you let the "shoulds" creep into your mind, you'll have a list that belongs to someone else, not truly yours.

You may be tempted to think about who you do NOT want. I urge you to avoid this train of thought. Remember, our subconscious cannot recognize negative directives. If you constantly think about what you do NOT want, you are still visualizing that object or situation. If you focus on avoiding the negative, you are essentially showing your subconscious an image of the negative and it will go to work for you to bring this to your life. When you focus only on what you DO want, your subconscious mind will work to get you there. Now that you have clearly defined the ideal you want, ask yourself an important follow up question:

Why do I want this _____ ?

Repeat the exercise, listing all the reasons why you want the characteristics you choose. Once you know what you want and why you want it, we can explore yet another very important question:

Why don't I have it right now?

When we are seeking a new goal, it is common for self-sabotaging beliefs to creep up and get in the way of our success. These beliefs can stem from the meaning we have placed on negative experiences or failures, the beliefs of others, and even childhood experiences.

They can be so deeply engraved in our subconscious that we may not be aware of the affect they have on our thoughts and behaviors. If you are wondering why you are having trouble or feel as if you've tried everything and nothing seems to work, it may be that you have some outdated beliefs that are keeping you right where you are. Here is where you dig deeply into your belief system!

List all the reasons (and excuses) you can come up with as to why you do not have this ideal _____ right now.

An example might look something like this:

'I just don't have the time'

'I just have too much going on right now'

'I'm not attractive enough so it's hard for me to get dates'

'I don't know where to get clients'

'All the good positions are already taken'

Now next to each reason, I want you to write down the belief behind this reason. An example might be something like this:

Reason: 'I just don't have the time right now'

Underlying Belief: 'Starting a business requires A LOT of time and other things in my life take up all of my extra time and are more important'

Reason: 'I'm not attractive enough so it's hard for me to get

22

dates'

Underlying Belief: 'Only really attractive people find dates easily' or 'you have to be a size X to be considered attractive' or 'Men prefer petite blondes and I don't look like that' or 'Women only want tall guys and I don't look like that'

Reason: 'I don't know where to get clients'

Underlying Belief: 'Successful and well-connected people get all the clients and I can't compete with that' or 'I don't have a large following like so-and so'

Reason: 'All the positions are already taken'

Underlying Belief: 'The good positions never come available since they're so desirable' or 'companies just aren't hiring these days'

You may be surprised to find some of the negative, self-sabotaging beliefs you have about yourself, about others, or the world in general. I challenge you to take each of these beliefs and ask yourself if they are true and/or if these beliefs are serving you.

Ask yourself the following questions and write down your answers for each of your beliefs:

Where did this belief come from? (Who did I learn this from? What experience led me to believe this?) Is it true or false?

What would happen if this belief were false?

What would happen if this belief were true?

How would I be different if this belief were false?

How would I be different if this belief were true?

These are all important questions to ask yourself. Be 100% honest! This is for you—your relationship, your happiness, and your lifestyle. No one except you will see these answers.

If you find a belief that is not based in reality or doesn't serve you in your current goal, negate it and replace it with one that is truthful, based in reality, and works with you in the present.

Do this for each self-sabotaging belief on your list. See what life changing principles you can create for yourself!

By doing this exercise, you are reframing the basic belief system from which you operate to attain your current objective. Connect with your subconscious (through meditation, yoga, self-hypnosis, etc.) and direct it with your newly framed beliefs.

Align your subconscious with your goals and new beliefs, tell it what you want and it will work for you to get you there! Let me give you another example of how negative beliefs can shape the relationships we have.

I've met with beautiful, intelligent women who consistently attract the manipulative types that take, take, and take from them but never give. These women are delightful souls who are nurturing and giving by nature—it's just who they are. They live to help others and they find joy in giving love and energy to others. Yet, they find themselves in relationships that never reciprocate their love and care. When these women have finally had enough and are ready to leave, the partner, friend, boss, etc., says 'all the right things' and influences them to stay.

These are the givers that are manipulated by the takers. Their underlying beliefs? Here are some common ones:

'I won't find a job better than this'

'I won't find anyone else better than this'

'There is something wrong with me'

'No one else will want me'

The dread of not being 'good enough', of not being worthy

is one of the greatest fears that humans have. This can keep us from moving forward, from attracting the right people to us and creating our ideal life. We stay stuck where we are, or if we leave an unhealthy situation, we continue to attract the identical 'type' because we hold onto the same mentality, the same behaviors and the same actions. This naturally creates the same results in our lives.

If you are stuck in this mentality ~ of being unworthy~ a fantastic way to BREAK OUT is to implement strong self-love exercises. Create a personal "brag book" for your eyes only. This brag book serves to open the mind, body, and spirit to all the wonderful, unique and valuable aspects of you.

If you don't have a brag book yet, get one! Make this exercise fun! Plan a trip to the store to pick out a special notebook with a color or design or feel that you love. If you enjoy typing more, create a special file folder for yourself on your mobile device or desktop.

In your brag book, list all the characteristics that you like about yourself. Then add compliments that friends, colleagues, and clients have given to you, thank you letters and awards you have received and achievements you have accomplished. Refer to this book at least once a week and as often as you need to.

Now, let's look at some examples that will help you negate and replace those self-sabotaging beliefs:

Example:

Self-sabotaging belief: 'I won't find a job better than this'

New belief: 'There are millions of companies in the world and technology has changed the way people work ~ my chances of finding one I want to work for is looking good!'

Self-sabotaging belief: 'I won't find anyone else better than this'

New belief: 'There are over 1 Billion people in the world and my chance of finding someone who will want to be with me and whom I want to be with is fantastic!'

Self-sabotaging belief: 'There is something wrong with me'

New belief: 'I am a valuable person who has a lot of love to give. I choose to give my love, talents, and knowledge only to those I see worthy of it.'

Self-sabotaging belief: 'No one else will want me'

New belief: 'I am a valuable person, worthy of love and respect'

Let me give you more examples...

I have also met with kind, easy going, and respectful men who have trouble finding their ideal partner. These types may get placed in the 'friend zone' or are taken advantage of for their financial success.

These men can't understand why they're not seen as a potential romantic partner instead of just a friend. Their income information is topic of discussion in the first few minutes of the first date. Why should that matter? It matters to those who are seeking to be financially dependent on them!

Here are some common beliefs that I hear:

'Women like bad boys, but that's just not me'

'Women only like rich guys'

'I've got to get into the gym before I can start dating again'

'I need to lose some weight before I start dating again'

'Nice guys finish last'

'I don't want to come across as too pushy'

'I don't want to scare them away'

'It's hard to go up to a woman and introduce yourself'

Again, the fear or not being 'good enough' creeps in. You can hear it in their voices and see it in their body language. It's even in the terminology that they use. They have those great qualities that women want—kind, supportive, easy-going, respectful, laid back, funny, and just pleasant to be around!

So why don't women take them seriously as a potential partner? Because they themselves don't believe they are good enough, and therefore they fail to convince others how awesome it is to be with them. They stay hidden.

Here are some examples of replacing that old belief with a new one that is based in reality and better serves:

Self-sabotaging belief: 'Women like bad boys, but that's just not me'

New belief: 'Women are attracted to confidence. Not only am I a confident man, but I have many wonderful qualities that women find attractive'

Self-sabotaging belief: 'Women only like the rich guys'

New belief: 'Women are attracted to responsible, goal-oriented, independent men who are resourceful and I am one of those men'

Self-sabotaging belief: 'I've got to get into the gym before I can start dating again'

New belief: 'Because I care about my well-being my health is important to me and I take care of myself physically'

Self-sabotaging belief: 'I've got to lose some weight before I start dating again'

New belief: 'My health is important to me and I take care of myself physically. My weight is a health factor, and does not determine my worth as a person'

Self-sabotaging belief: 'Nice guys finish last'

New belief: 'People gravitate towards nice guys because they are enjoyable to be around'

Self-sabotaging belief: 'I don't want to come across as too pushy'

New belief: 'I am authentic in my communication and speak with kindness and assertiveness'

Self-sabotaging belief: 'I don't want to scare them away'

New belief: 'I am authentic in my communication which allows for others to feel comfortable around me'

Self-sabotaging belief: 'It's hard to go up to a woman and introduce yourself'

New belief: 'I am a person of value and I have a lot of love to give. I confidently introduce myself to those I am interested in meeting'

This reframing process is extremely powerful. It doesn't matter how long you've had your self-sabotaging beliefs, they can be changed in an instant. Forget about the past, forget about what happened on the last date, last relationship, last time you felt embarrassed or frustrated ...focus on the present and focus on moving forward to create the life you want. When we dwell on the negative parts of the past, we are hindering ourselves in the present.

Mindset work is powerful! And yet mindset work is only one piece of the puzzle:

Thought—Behavior—Action—Result

Yes, it is true that all change begins in the mind, yet when you begin to think about yourself differently and see yourself in a different light, you will also begin to behave differently. Others will notice your behavior and your overall presence.

What is your presence when you walk into a room?

Your presence, your demeanor, is a big part of how others perceive you—how you dress, your personal style, how you walk, talk and act, how you carry yourself, your posture, your mannerisms, your overall body language. Your own personal style, your 'vibe' is an important communication signal that you send to the world.

If your outward presence isn't aligned with the message you wish to send, and you are not getting the feedback you desire, then there is a disconnect that you need to address.

4 STRATEGY #2 DEVELOP YOUR SELF-IMAGE VERSION 2.0

Closing the gap between you and your ideal self

If you are a daydreamer like I am, you have probably dreamed of the person you would like to be. Perhaps you have dreamed of the best version of you, with all the characteristics you admire. You have dreamed of how you would talk, walk, dress, and interact with others. You have dreamed of the relationships you would enjoy, a career you would be proud of, and living a perfect lifestyle to suit your tastes. You have dreamed how others would speak of you, of the strong impact you could have on their lives.

Maybe you think about this best self often, but it feels out of reach. We often give ourselves many excuses for the gap between expectation and reality:

'If I had more time'
'If I only had the willpower'
'If I didn't have so much going on right now'
'If I weren't so afraid'
'If I were more confident in myself'
'If I had more money'
'If I had done things differently in the past'

If you are not projecting the image you would like, don't fret —I have very good news for you—you have the power to change that! Let me share a story with you...

I once coached a woman who was struggling with her self-image. She was feeling dull, frumpy, and unattractive. She was a brilliant woman—highly intelligent, very accomplished, and confident in her work, yet her self-image suffered because she did not feel like her authentic self.

As we went deeper into conversation, I asked her a very important question: "What is the ideal image you want to portray?"

She vividly described an elegant, graceful dancer who seemed to float across the room effortlessly ~ the type that could walk into a room and catch everyone's attention. I began to visualize and understand the dancer as she described this woman who was confident, poised, refined and had a striking presence.

When I asked her why she was not this person now, she listed her reasons. Many of them pertained to her style of clothing, some unwanted weight she had gained, and the fact that she had not been active in quite some time due to the stress of work. These all were holding her back from the journey to her ideal self.

Further into our discussion, I found that due to a financial burden a family member had placed upon her, she had given up something which she very much enjoyed ~ dancing lessons. When she was dancing she felt graceful, the flow of energy allowed her to be in tune with her body and she felt very feminine. It became clear to both of us that she needed to resume her dancing lessons!

Once she started dancing again, she regained the connection between her mind and body. She noticed a change in her physique, which sparked new enthusiasm for updating her wardrobe and having fun styling herself! This energy carried through to the way she interacted with others and her image completely changed from dull and frumpy to bright, confident, and graceful! She now walks into any work or social event with full confidence, able to mix and mingle effortlessly with those in the room.

Becoming your ideal self begins with a simple choice—that you are no longer going to let excuses get in the way of what you want.

At the time in my life when I made the decision to leave an abusive relationship, I was single again but not feeling like myself. I hardly recognized the person in the mirror. I looked and felt tired, sluggish, sloppy, insecure and sad.

This was not my authentic self and certainly not the image I wanted to portray to others. I thought about the person that I wanted to be—bright, happy, laughing, generous, warm, sophisticated, stylish, healthy, and confident. It had been quite some time since I felt like that person.

I decided I was tired of looking in the mirror and not recognizing the woman staring back at me. I began to implement changes that helped me transform into my authentic self. I started working out again, I started saying yes to every social invitation I received—I began meeting new people and making new friends.

I tried some new sports (tennis and golf) and took up some new hobbies (Pilates and reading for fun, not work). I read and read and read! My life started to become full of laughter, friendship, growth and new adventures. It felt good! I felt like I was living again! And it all started with daydreaming about the best version of myself—the person I wanted to be.

Give yourself permission to daydream for a few minutes; sit in a quiet place where you can allow yourself to think. As you do, write down your answers to the following questions:

Envision your best self—what are the specific qualities you admire?

How does your best self think, what do you say, and do?

What do you admire about this best self?

How does he/she make you feel?

WHY do you want to be this person?

What is stopping you from being this person now?

Most importantly: what must happen for you to become this person?

Think about your best self in terms of relationships. What sort of partner do you want to be? What sort of friend do you want to be? What sort of parent, sibling, mentor, teacher, business associate, neighbor, or colleague do you want to be?

Your answers to these questions will provide you with insights and with the actions that you need to take to become your ideal self.

Place your own mask on before assisting others

We know that self-love is important ~ why do we not practice it consistently?

The start of a beautiful relationship with another person begins with self-love. Self-love means loving yourself no matter what. It means respecting yourself. It means taking care of yourself physically, mentally, emotionally, and spiritually. It means being your own best friend, your own cheerleader, and your own support system FIRST. It means fulfilling your basic human needs yourself BEFORE asking others to fulfill them for you.

When we practice self-love on a daily basis, it becomes a strong habit and that habit becomes a lifestyle.

If you are struggling with developing a practice of self-love, here are some methods you can implement immediately:

Start paying attention to self-dialogue

How do you talk to yourself?

There may be times throughout the day where you scold, criticize or relay negative messages to yourself without even realizing it! The first step is to recognize these moments. Do you see a pattern? Is there a similar time of day, a certain person or group you are around, or a particular situation in which you use negative self-talk?

I recommend writing these down in a notebook or journal as they happen. By recording them daily, weekly, and monthly, you can analyze your patterns of self-talk. Can you image what YEARS of negative self-talk does to your self-esteem, self-image and your confidence? To your life?

I cannot tell you how many clients have created big changes in their life simply by recognizing negative self-talk and stopping it in its tracks!

I once had the privilege of coaching a kind-hearted man who was a consultant. This man was a perfectionist and put an enormous amount of pressure on himself to consistently deliver excellence to his clients. Before meetings, he would become so nervous that he literally got sick to his stomach. He compared himself to other consultants, much older and more experienced than he, who 'always seemed to know the right answers'—always knew what to do, what to say, and how to help their clients.

His biggest fear was that he wouldn't be able to perform as they did ~ that he would fail his clients by not living up to his own expectations. Throughout the day, he would engage in negative self-talk and self-doubt, which set the frame for how his day would go. He was beginning to self-sabotage his meetings with clients, appearing nervous and unsure of himself and his abilities.

In one of our coaching sessions, I asked him to describe positive feedback he had received from past clients. There were some wonderful comments about the value of his work and the constructive impact he had on their lives!

The best thing you can do to combat fear is to stop focusing on yourself, and focus on serving others.

Once he began to recognize his negative self-talk and stopped it he began to get out of his head and into his heart—

focusing on his client's well-being. We explored ways in which he could set the frame for each meeting by preparing himself for the day. He developed a morning ritual for himself, saying a prayer and reading his personal mission statement out loud before he met with a client. What happened? He crushed it! Client success stories and feedback came quickly. He attained a secure confidence in himself and in his capability to meet and out-perform his goals. The satisfaction of knowing he was helping his clients created a 'calm excitement' within him and he no longer felt inadequate.

Take Control. Make a promise to yourself that only positive self-talk is allowed and notice the changes that begin to take place! This is a big one. I cannot express enough how much your life will improve when you change that internal voice from negative to positive.

Nourish, Exercise, and Rest

These seem like no-brainers, but you'd be surprised how many people don't do these things as often as they could. You only get one body in this lifetime, so take loving care of it!

~Nourish: The cells in your body are constantly growing, working, and repairing themselves. Feed your body nutritious food that fuels cells and gives you energy!

~Exercise: Challenge your body so it can grow stronger. Exercise your muscles, get your blood pumping, achieve that flood of endorphins! Find an exercise that you love ~ dancing, yoga, walking, jogging, playing a sport with friends, lifting weights, etc. Make sure you enjoy it, otherwise you won't stick with it!

~Rest: Allow your body to rest, repair and rejuvenate itself. Don't get enough of this? Without enough sleep you're more prone to things like injury, cloudy thinking, less that optimal performance, and negative behaviors.

Making a strong effort to frequently nourish, exercise, and rest your body will make you feel good! When you feel good, you look good! Your inner radiance shines through...in your eyes...in your smile... in your overall body language.

When you feel good AND look good, your confidence is through the roof! When you have confidence, you can do some pretty amazing things!

Some of you probably think 'yea, I already know all that' and go on with your week, falling into the trap of what I call "knowing your way out of it". You already know these things, but you don't DO THEM.

Some of you will take action! You will create a personal plan, incorporating it into your daily routine ~ eventually it becomes habit, and you will see the benefits physical self-care has on your confidence.

Tip: When you let yourself rest and are in a peaceful state of mind, you increase the opportunity for your creativity to flow. This is especially helpful for those who are writers, artists, or who are starting a business or transitioning into a new career. Ideas tend to pop up when you are in this creative flow! I do my best brainstorming when I am sitting in a coffee shop with decor I love, soothing music playing, completely relaxed (latte in hand). That is my perfect environment for my flow state. What is yours? If you don't have one yet, find or create your unique environment and visit it whenever you need to unleash your creativity and generate new ideas! You can create this space in your home too. Grab a copy of Joanna Gaines's design book and get to work on your special room or nook for creativity. Chanel your inner Marie Kondo and get to work creating clear and organized spaces. Happy decorating!

Allow yourself to express your emotions

We are human beings—It's normal to feel emotions!

When we don't express our emotions, or "bottle them up inside", we carry that tension in our bodies. The body can only remain in a tense state for so long until it must find release—

often at an inconvenient time for us. When this happens, it is usual to become embarrassed or ashamed about our lack of control over our emotions and that's often when negative self-talk begins.

Whether the emotions are joy, excitement, sadness, anger, etc., give yourself the proper time to feel them and express them in positive ways.

A note about anger—anger gets a bad rap, but anger is an important emotion when listened to and channeled correctly. Anger helps alert us. It helps us recognize when we need to protect ourselves and make a change. If channeled correctly, anger can become a huge motivating factor in creating amazing changes in our lives. It can give us the courage to do what needs to be done.

How Body Image Affects Our Relationships & Career Success

Recently in the media, there has been a lot of talk about body image and how it affects our health.

What is body image?

The dictionary defines it as "a subjective picture of one's own physical appearance established both by self-observation and by noting the reactions of others".

According to a study in the Journal of Sex Research, "Women's relationship status is directly related to their subjective view of themselves and their sexual self-esteem, not to their actual body size, or the objective researchers' rating of their physical attractiveness."

What does this mean?

It means that you are in control of your own beauty. If you think, feel, and act as if you are beautiful, then you are! This sort of behavior is so very attractive. Think about it—no one wants to be around someone who is constantly putting themselves down. It makes for an awkward situation and is unpleasant for the listener.

Each of us have characteristics that make us uniquely beautiful. So if you are waiting around for someone else to tell you you're beautiful, please stop. Take a look in the mirror and notice your beauty. Talk to yourself many times throughout the day to tell yourself that you are beautiful. Take time to notice the unique beautiful features that you have—the things that make you special.

Is this starting to sound a little narcissistic? Good! Maybe you need a little more narcissism and a lot less negative self-talk. When you feel and act beautiful, it magnifies other people's view of your beauty.

What does having a positive body image mean to you?

How does having a negative body image influence your life?

How does having a positive body image influence your life?

How do you think it affects the quality of your relationships?

Don't just think, write it down. Get the words on paper. If you're one of those people who knows they are beautiful but think, "Men/Women only like _____ ", let me stop you right there.

I once coached a tall, slim, dark-haired beauty who said she had trouble attracting men. She had a fun personality and was open to dating but couldn't seem to get a date. She sat at bars or in restaurants, waiting for men to come over and talk to her. No one would approach her. Her male friends told her that she was 'unapproachable' or that she 'looked too serious'.

This frustrated her even more because she was completely open and willing to have a conversation with someone! She wanted a man to come over and introduce himself. She was the one scanning the room, trying to make eye contact!

When I asked her to name some beautiful, famous women, she described a few dark-haired actresses. I asked her if she thought she was beautiful and she said yes, but with a sigh, stated, "Men seem to only like petite blondes".

I asked her where she had gotten this information. I found out that when she was younger, her petite, blonde sister received a lot of attention from the guys at school and around the neighborhood. They were very attentive to her sister but ignored her. It was clear how she had developed this belief many years ago that men only liked petite blondes.

Do you see how your old beliefs can hurt you in the present? Her outdated, self-sabotaging belief was literally killing her chances of finding a companion decades later.

Though she knew that there were many beautiful, dark-haired, and tall actresses who were sought after by millions of men —she still could not let go of the meaning she has assigned to her teenage experience. She believed she was beautiful but also believed that men would not find her attractive. This inner conflict was driving her nuts!

So what did I do? I told her about the tropical paradise and bustling city of Miami. I told her about the vibrant culture in south Florida and the different perceptions of beauty that I had witnessed living there. She was astounded...

"Really??!" "Yes, really"

It blew her mind that not everyone desired one type of woman—the petite blonde. I have nothing against petite blondes.... they are beautiful too! But there are many different forms of beauty. The saying: "Beauty is in the eye of the beholder" couldn't be more true.

We went further, abolished her old, outdated belief and replaced it with a new one that was based in reality and better served her in the present. I can't tell you the results of the session, because her homework assignment was quite interesting, but I will say her perception changed completely and I sensed a new confidence and enthusiasm as she got up to leave!

5 STRATEGY #3 UNLEASH YOUR PERSONAL POWER

Use your energy to attract and repel the right people into your life

Having the right people in your life is joyful and fulfilling! Having the wrong ones can be frustrating, exhausting, and can feel quite lonely. A friend who is supportive, positive and compassionate will give you energy and bring joy to your life. A client who is negative, pushy, demanding, and entitled will drain your energy and leave you tired, which in turn makes it hard to serve your other clients and give attention to the loved ones in your life.

I often hear the phrase "I always attract the weirdos", or "I always attract the takers", meaning the creepy, weird, controlling, abusive, lazy, or manipulative types. If this is you, I can certainly relate.

There was a time in my life when I felt I had a large target on my back saying, "Here I am weirdos, come bother me!". My experiences had led me to believe that there was always a hidden agenda behind a nice smile.

Thankfully, I learned the truth—there are many genuine people out there who are sincerely looking to connect and share their gifts with you, and there are also those with a negative, concealed agenda. The more often I came across the latter, the better I became at recognizing the signs.

I found that when I shifted my energy, things changed dramatically for me. Let me share with you my experience of altering energies, of revising the 'vibe' I was sending out. It is not 100% foolproof—it's not a guarantee that you will never come across another weirdo or manipulator. However, I promise you that once I made this adjustment myself, I began to see dramatic results in the type of people I was attracting and also in those that appealed to me. It was so refreshing!

Let me share a personal story with you:

I was once in an abusive relationship. Before I met this man, I had gone through a traumatic experience which left me quite vulnerable emotionally. This was the time I attracted my abusive partner. I went from being a high achiever, a fun, lively and happy person to being a controlled, depressed, lifeless victim. My best friends and family noticed the change in me. I faked it. I told them I was ok. That's what people tend to do in abusive relationships—they lie because they're embarrassed, or in denial, or in fear. For me, it was all three of these.

One day, after a terrible incident with him, I had an instant breakthrough. The proverbial lightbulb went off in my brainwashed head! It was extremely bizarre—how remarkable to look back on it now and realize that this tiny moment was the turning point in reclaiming my life. Sometimes an instant of complete clarity occurs and it brings about a life transforming shift.

At that moment, I realized that if I stayed in this relationship, it would destroy what little of myself was left. I would be completely dead inside, my self-esteem completely gone. I loved myself enough to decide that I would not stay with him. I wasn't sure how or when, but I was going to remove myself from this situation, or in my own words at the time: "Get the hell out!"

With the help of some caring friends (angels really!), I found the means to leave the relationship. Once free and safe, I began dating again. What do you think happened? I found myself attracting and dating the SAME controlling, angry, and insecure type of men!

The very things I had escaped from.... anger management issues, money management issues, control issues, jealousy, and alcohol problems were coming right back at me!

I immediately stopped dating. At this point, I was truly discouraged. I couldn't believe this was happening to me AGAIN!

I felt hopeless...I would never find someone kind and caring~ someone who would treat me with the love and respect that I deserved.

One day I got a phone call from my ex, abusive partner. He began to scream at me over the phone, bullying and intimidating me. He wanted to know where I was living. When I refused to tell him, he became angrier and louder; he threatened to show up at my place of work and slash the tires on my car if I didn't tell him where I lived.

In that moment, something inside of me snapped. It was the warrior who had been sleeping. She was wide-awake now! Maybe this was my body in survival mode? Maybe I reached the point where I could no longer suppress this part of myself?

She yelled back and went on the offense! She stood up for me and helped me regain my personal power. She told him that if he showed up at my workplace, the police would be called and all my co-workers would help to make sure he was taken away!

He instantly backed down. Why? Because that's what bullies do when they know they can no longer control you (and they want to avoid jail!).

It was another breakthrough that I genuinely needed!

After that phone call, there was no more abuse. This was the beginning of the end of my victim mentality. I started my transformation and began to regain my personal power.

I felt strong and confident. Most importantly, I was back to my true nature—a happy, fun, and kind person with lots of joy and love to give! My inner "light" was renewed and beginning to shine again!

Soon, something interesting happened. I met a wonderful,

kind, generous and confident young man who would later become my husband. I attracted what I wanted, what I was truly seeking: confidence, generosity and kindness. He was drawn to me because of my loving and easygoing nature.

The negative, victim vibe was washing away and my inner light could show through. It was loving, easygoing, kind, fun, playful, and STRONG!

Some people may wonder, why didn't she teach the bad guy to be loving and kind? Why didn't she heal him?

The short answer is that I tried, many times. I aim to see the best in every person. However, when you are being mentally, emotionally and physically abused, the only answer is to get out of the situation for your personal safety.

If you are in a circumstance like this, do not try to 'fix' the abuser... the longer you stay, the greater your chance of being hurt more extremely than you may have already been. Many women end up in the hospital or tragically, worse.

I am very lucky I got out before it got that far. My advice is to leave, move on, and pray for them. Pray that they find the help and enlightenment that they so desperately need.

Please know that the negative actions of another person are NOT your fault. You cannot control the thoughts, behaviors, or actions of another person.

What you can control is your ability to attract the type of people you want to be with. People are drawn to or repelled by energy. The 'vibe' you put out is a result of your thoughts. If you think you are a victim, you will continue to tell the story of the victim and continue to live it out.

If believe in your personal power, you will do powerful things, you will make things happen!

If you think you are a joyful person, your energy will be expressed at joy and you'll spread it to others.

Our thoughts determine our behaviors, our behaviors determine our actions, and our actions produce results.

Thought—Behavior—Action—Result

If you want to change the results in your life, change your

thoughts. If you find yourself continually attracting the wrong type of man or woman, think of possible reasons this is happening.

I was extremely insecure, therefore I attracted insecure, controlling manipulators. Why were these manipulators attracted to me? What did they sense when they looked at me? A potential victim.

Often, excessive givers are surrounded by extreme takers. Desperate individuals attract those who will take advantage. Those with low self-esteem are a target for abusers and users.

Pay attention to the actions of others (not just the words), notice the patterns and be aware of the energy you are projecting. This goes for all aspects of your life—not just romantic relationships—but in the workplace, in your business networking, your community engagements, etc.

Very importantly, listen to your intuition. If something does not seem right, ask yourself why. Your intuition is there to help protect you—use it!

Let's move on to a more positive note...

Shine bright like a diamond

We all have natural strengths and gifts to share with the world. We are each unique: with natural talents, personalities, and an attractive magnetism. By attractive magnetism I don't mean physical appearance, but rather the unique inner 'light' that you have ~ that spark that naturally draws others to you.

It is a joy that others feel when they are around you and it emanates from the joy you feel in your heart. Some might call it an 'aura', or a 'vibe'. No matter the way you phrase it, it is the very essence of you.

When this essence of you shines through, when you practice self-love frequently, when you open yourself to loving others, your inner radiance sparkles! Others can see it, feel it, and sense it.

Think of someone that you truly enjoy being around. Is there an undefinable 'something' that draws you to them?

Perhaps it's just a general feeling you get when you're in their presence? These types of people are authentic, confident in themselves, and open to giving and receiving love.

They are good at 'hearing' others and they enable people to feel worthy by taking the time to listen and understand them. Their words, body language, and actions allow others to feel comfortable in expressing themselves. Their 'light' shines brightly, warmly and attracts others to them.

I knew a lady (sadly she recently passed away) who was a prime example of what it means to allow your inner light to shine. She was the wife of a distant relative and the first time I met her, I instantly liked her. She was glowing!

She was a beautiful woman in her 60's who had taken care of her body, mind, and spirit. She looked much younger than her age, and her personality was a kind, happy, and bubbly one.

I loved talking to her because I always left the conversation feeling good. She had a kind soul and always looked at the positive in everyone and everything.

In the brief time that I knew her, I learned that she spent much time focused on health, spirituality, mindset work, and spreading love and joy. 'Love and joy' were major themes in her life—they were even the focus of her children's books and songs.

Everywhere she went, people loved her. She made a significant impact on many lives just by being herself! I attended her funeral, and was astonished at the number of people who came to mourn her loss.

One by one, people stood up to speak about her ~ it was evident that I was not the only one whose life had been deeply touched by her inner light of love and joy.

She taught me three major lessons: Love, Joy and Light

Love

Be loving to yourself and to others. Love yourself and know that YOU ARE GOOD. Give love to others, spread the love, and always look for the good in every situation.

Joy, joy, joy!

That was her motto, one that she shared with others. Think joyful thoughts, be joyful, share joy with others. Stop negative thoughts in their tracks and replace them with joyful ones.

Be a light for others

A letter written by her husband described her as the light that had brought him out of darkness. And she was ~ a light for many people. She was certainly a light for my late grandmother who (bless her heart) struggled with worry, fear, anger, and resentment. My grandmother would get herself very worked up over an issue, and then remember to use her motto, "Joy, joy, joy" to calm herself and keep things in perspective.

Each of us is unique and when we allow our 'inner light' to shine, we are being our authentic selves, sharing our special gift with others. It is then that we naturally attract pleasant people to us—it feels effortless because it's genuine.

How do you allow your "inner light" to shine? It begins with self-love and ends with shifting the focus from you, towards helping others.

Snap into it! How to call out your inner Goddess or Warrior

Each of us have a 'core' energy. As women, we are all feminine on a deep level, regardless our style of dress, who we desire sexually or how we act. The same goes for men—all have masculinity at their core.

Some wrongly associate feminine energy with being "weak". On the contrary, feminine energy has strength in many ways: Feminine energy is about 'flow'...intuition, giving freely, nurturing, creating. The love of a wife or mother is a powerful force that creates positive effects.

Some wrongly associate masculine energy with anger, tyranny, or being bossy. Masculine energy is strong yet kind. It is protective; it is present and loyal no matter what happens. An excellent metaphor to describe masculine energy is: 'like a rock'—steady amid a storm. It is also ultra focused on a singular task.

Each of us have feminine and masculine energies that we need to call upon in different situations. We each need the flow, playful spontaneity to brainstorm and create and the calm, present, laser-focused to take action and get things done! Just think back to the caveman days—women had to socialize, to cooperate, to build the community, so the families could grow and thrive. Men had to protect, hunt and gather, otherwise the families would starve. Men had to be ultra focused on the singular task at hand, any distractions and they might miss the kill. You have both energies within you and both will help you to achieve your goals. You just need to know when to call upon each when the situation dictates.

Sometimes you need that feminine energy to brainstorm, create, flow, cooperate, negotiate, and other times you need that masculine energy to focus, take action, achieve, stand up for yourself, weather the storm, and get things done.

How do you shift energies? What methods do you use? How long do those methods take? Wouldn't it be wonderful if you could just flip a switch...if you could shift energies in a matter of seconds?

If you have difficulty transitioning to feminine energy, here is a method you may find helpful:

Choose a symbol or metaphor that is ultra-feminine to you. It may be a picture of you in a girly dress, a pink fabric swatch, a whimsical sound, a piece of delicate jewelry, or an image of a soft flower, etc.

Select something that categorically represents 'feminine' for you. You must have that strong an association for your metaphor to work for you.

When you need to shift into your feminine energy, take a few deep breaths and allow your body to slip into a relaxed state. When you are calm and ready, look at your metaphor, hold it in your hand, touch it, listen to it, experience it.

Feel your energy drift into 'flow'—an easygoing, playful,

creative energy. Practice, practice, practice. Once you have mastered this method, you'll be able to simply close your eyes and visualize it. You'll have the ability to 'flip the switch' anywhere, at any time by visualizing your metaphor.

The same can be done for masculine metaphors when you need to call upon your masculine energy. (I tend to think of "Eye of the Tiger" and Rocky training before his fight)

Practice shifting between feminine and masculine energies and you'll be able to utilize each when the situation calls for it.

6 STRATEGY #4 NURTURE YOUR CONFIDENCE

Confidence is appealing in numerous ways. To have confidence does not mean to live without fear; it means believing in yourself and having the courage to overcome obstacles in the presence of fear. It means to be boldly be yourself, regardless of the judgement of others. This is true confidence.

Before we go further, let's review the differences between confidence, self-esteem, and self-image:

Self-esteem: Your overall perception of your own worth and value—your self-concept. The way you think about yourself.

Self-image: Your opinion of your own abilities, appearance, and personality.

Self-confidence: A feeling of self-assurance based upon your appreciation of your own abilities or qualities.

Recognizing True Confidence

People can fake confidence, you most often see it in the form of arrogance. Frequently, arrogant people are the least confident ~they are hiding behind a facade they have created to prevent others from finding out the truth.

They put on an outward show of false confidence because they are terrified of rejection and judgement. They feel very unworthy of love and they put extra effort into fabricating a persona that gives them a false sense of security--a mask, if you will.

These people usually appear popular, but often they have very few, if any TRUE friends. If this is you, please know that you don't need a mask. You can give yourself permission to be yourself! Stop hiding and start living—Truly living! You will feel so free, I promise!

Genuine confidence is extremely attractive. It draws others to you. Most people like to be around confident people….it allows them to feel safe, comfortable, excited, hopeful, and happy.

Yet others avoid confident people because it makes them feel uncomfortable, jealous, or envious. They feel that they themselves pale by comparison.

They long for such self-assurance and it pains them to be around those that are so unaffected by the judgements of others.

A note here about 'playing The Comparison Game':

The comparison game is a game you CANNOT and WILL NOT win.

No matter how beautiful, intelligent, athletic, skilled, or wealthy you are—there is always someone out there who has more. This is a dangerous, self-destructive game that I urge you not to play. There are never any winners in this game.

Some people will admire and support your confidence, others who are threatened by it will try to break it down.

Find people who admire and support your confidence— these are the people that you want surrounding you, these are the ones with whom you can have happy and healthy relationships.

A colleague once told me an interesting story about AA (Alcoholics Anonymous). She said the first thing that they tell their attendees is: if you want to quit drinking and change your life, you need a new set of friends.

My initial, reactive thought was: No, change comes from within. You are responsible for your actions, you can't blame your alcoholism on your closest friends. Then I realized that to change your life, you not only have to change from within, you must also change your environment. The two go hand-in-hand.

When you surround yourself with those who have the values and qualities you respect, your subconscious mind gathers information from your environment and goes to work for you —eventually you find yourself emulating those values and qualities.

Giving up your role as chief people pleaser

Do you find that some of your stress comes from worrying about what others think of you? Are you constantly trying to "keep up with the Joneses"? Does the idea of being judged by others influence your decisions, behaviors, actions? Do you sometimes feel that you are living a life that someone else has created for you? Do you sacrifice your interests, time, energy and personal relationships for people you really don't care for and then wonder, "Why am I doing this again?"

Are you a YES person?

What would happen to you if you stepped down from your role of chief people pleaser?

What would that do for your self-esteem, your self-image and your confidence?

How can you grow towards your best self if you're constantly worrying about what others think of you?

Let go of the worry. If someone doesn't think you are interesting, pretty, smart, cool, stylish, or successful, that's ok— move along. Living your life on someone else's terms slowly eats away at your soul. It's a horrible way to live!

Quite frankly, it's not really living—it's following indirect orders from someone else. Once you stop worrying about what others think, you will be free to think for yourself and to work towards making things happen for you!

Model your confident self

Self-confident people inspire trust in others: their peers, friends, children, colleagues, clients, etc. Gaining the trust of others is one of the ways in which self-assured people find success. If you don't feel confident, I have good news for you—self-confidence can be learned and will increase with effort.

How do I become confident when I'm not?

A key step toward building confidence is to "do". Practice behaviors and actions that your confident self would do, until they are second nature. Think back to your description of your best self that you developed in Chapter 4. Ask yourself the following questions:

If I were my ideal self, full of confidence, what would I do?

How would I behave?

Would I act differently?

When you begin to emulate your confident self, you get closer and closer to complete and true confidence.

Confidence comes from repetition—when we do something again and again many times, it becomes natural. Think about sports for example. Pro athletes practice the same movements over and over thousands of times. It doesn't mean they never get nervous before a game or match, but they've done it so many times before that they are confident in their abilities to perform.

Confidence begins to develop when you begin taking

ACTION.

Growing Your Confidence Bank

This exercise is what I call Growing Your Confidence Bank (GYCB)

Write down a list of actions your confident self would carry out. Don't stop until you have an extensive list. The longer your list, the more opportunities you have to invest in your Confidence Bank Account. Once you have completed your list, put a dollar value next to each item. The more valuable the behavior is to you, the higher dollar value you place on it. For example:

1. Starting a conversation with a stranger in public - $25
2. Speaking publicly at an event - $100
3. Asking a love interest for a coffee date - $50
4. Running a 5k race - $80
5. Sky Diving - $1,000 (eh, maybe $5,000!)
6. Hiring a personal trainer who will help you reach your ultimate fitness goals- $125

Most people are going to cringe at the next part, but remember that you want to be 'confidence rich'!
Each week, choose ONE item on your list and do it. This will ease your fears and you will come to know the truth—that you can take action!
Every time you conquer a fear, your ability to overcome obstacles grows stronger. You develop resilience—an important characteristic that is found in highly successful people. You will learn that whatever comes your way, you can 'figure it out' because you are resourceful.
Your Confidence Bank account grows and grows! Each conquered item on your list is a further investment in your confidence.
Pretty soon you'll have a nice large bank account that you can draw from whenever you need to because you have become

confidence rich!

R-E-S-P-E-C-T

RESPECTING YOURSELF AND YOUR TIME

Confident people respect themselves.

Think about the way you speak to yourself, and how you take care of yourself: physically, mentally, emotionally, and spiritually. This is an important topic for those of you who give your all to your children, spouses, siblings, parents, and friends and often feel guilty if you do anything for yourself.

Before you can give your best care to others, you must be at your best. You cannot be at your best, if you do not take good care of yourself. Remember the phrase "You can't pour from an empty cup".

This means giving yourself time to rest, time to exercise, time to eat, time to have fun, time to think, time to create, and time devoted to your religious or spiritual beliefs.

A large part of respecting yourself is valuing your personal TIME. Ever heard the phrase "you teach others how to treat you?". I have found this to be quite true! If you don't respect your own time, how can you expect the same from others? I'll share a funny story with you...

One of my girlfriends told me the story of when she and her husband met and began dating. They had plans to get together one evening.... she was scheduled to meet him at his apartment at 7:00 that evening. She got caught up with some things, and was running an hour late. When she arrived she found the door locked, so she knocked. No answer. She stood outside knocking and knocking for a few minutes. Still no answer at the door.

She phoned and told him that she was standing outside and asked him to answer the door. He said to her that she was over an hour late and if she could not respect his time, then he would not share it with her. She was appalled!

After arguing with him on the phone for a few minutes, she got in her car and drove home. She was so upset! She had driven 45 minutes to get to his apartment only to turn right around and go back home!

How could he do this to her? How embarrassing!

But do you know what she told me? She was never again late when meeting him. And she realized that he was right—she needed to honor his time as he honored hers. He had taught her a very important lesson—how to respect him and his time.

A while ago I realized how much I was allowing others to waste my time:

I had a colleague who was very self-serving. I found myself spending about an hour a day, both in person, and on the phone after work listening to her talk, talk, talk about herself, about others, and about things that were of little interest to me. These conversations were not adding any value to my life, and they usually weren't even enjoyable. Once I stopped taking part in the conversations, I found I had an extra hour in my day!

One extra hour to do whatever I wanted! I could go to the gym, I could read that book I had been wanting to read for a long time. I could practice my French lessons, I could take up the violin, I could even take a nap! Oh the possibilities!

Respect your time, do not allow others to waste it and you will be amazed. Your time is precious, do not squander it.

You can always acquire more money, more material things, but you never get more time.

Portraying your confidence

The most confident people can walk into a room and people notice their 'presence'. They need not speak of their credentials, achievements, assets or status because they do not worry about the judgement of others. They know who they are and they hold their own space.

A lion doesn't need to tell you he is a lion.

When mingling in a group of new people, do you find yourself wanting to allude to your credentials? Do you feel that you need to gain the respect of others by notifying them of your title or education? Or are you comfortable just talking and holding your own space because you're YOU?

The first impression you make on others is 50% visual, 30% auditory, and 20% actual words.

Visual: When we look at others, we innately search for signs of self-care.

Does this person take care of themselves?

Is your body weight healthy and appropriate for your height and age? Do you exhibit good personal hygiene, modernly styled and well-groomed hair? Do you have clear and clean skin and nails? If you wear makeup, is it even and polished? Does it enhance your natural beauty or mask it?

Your appearance communicates a message to others (i.e., whether you're lazy or ambitious, up to date or out of touch, clean or dirty, organized or disheveled). Often, if you are facing mental roadblocks, are overwhelmed or confused, it's a sign that you need to focus on cleansing yourself and your home so that you can move forward with clarity and direction.

People will always notice how you dress. You don't have to break the bank on your wardrobe, but wear items that are attractive, stylish and well put together. Your clothing style reflects you in many ways! It is a creative outlet of self-expression! Have fun with it!

Don't think for a second that you must be ultra-wealthy to look nice and be well put together. I've known people who always look like a million bucks though their bank account didn't reflect that and I've known wealthy people who look sloppy and disheveled.

Auditory: Think about the voice you use when communicating with others…. notice the pitch, tone, and pace. Is your voice vibrant, passionate, soothing or monotone? Does your voice indicate confidence or do you sound unsure of yourself?

Voices make you 'feel'. Think about the voice of Morgan Freeman... what sort of feelings do they awake? Think of your favorite speakers, singers, or those you just love listening to. Describe their voices. What do you enjoy about them?

Our voices are quite powerful!

Speak clearly and with authority to command the attention of others. If you want help in developing your confident voice, a wonderful place to start is with a voice coach.

Words: Increase your vocabulary so you can adequately express yourself. Words cannot be taken back so choose them wisely. Once they leave your mouth, they are out there!

7 STRATEGY #5 TAKE CONTROL OF YOUR TIME AND ENERGY

Who is in your inner circle?

Your circle of friends plays a vital role in shaping who you are, what you do, and ultimately how successful you become. If you surround yourself with positive and successful people, you will be positive and successful. If you surround yourself with negative complainers, you will find yourself becoming one.

Some people call it their 'tribe' or 'inner circle', in business relationships it is often referred to as a 'mastermind' group. Whatever term you choose, it's your environment ~ make sure it supports authenticity, positivity, and growth.

Taking the time to evaluate your tribe is time well spent. List the 5-10 people with whom you have the most contact on a daily or weekly basis.

After each name, note if they are supportive or not supportive of your personal confidence.

Some of you may happily notice that you are surrounded by positive and supporting people!

Others might look at your inner circle and realize you need to make some changes!

It is extremely difficult to acknowledge that someone in your circle is not a positive influence, especially if they are a close friend or a family member. I have had to remove people from my inner circle who were bringing massive negativity and pain to my life.

It was a very difficult thing to do, but once done, I instantly felt relieved. Soon I began to see positive changes in my personal relationships, my health, and my business.

It can also be a powerful wake up call for those 'negative nancies' who need to change their ways.

If there is an unsupportive person you are unable to avoid (such as a boss or family member), find a way to bolster your personal strength when you are in their presence.

Recognizing that this person has a negative influence on your confidence is the first step. Know that whatever negativity they project is a result of their own way of thinking…. understand that it is their problem.

This is great practice for you! As you continue to master this skill, you will be able to use it whenever you come across a person who challenges your confidence.

When you are on a path of growth and you're gaining momentum towards your goals, you will come across variables that will test you. Negative people, setbacks, and obstacles can appear out of nowhere ~ your job is to protect your mindset. Turn these outside variables into opportunities for growth and change.

Have you noticed how successful people tend to keep company with other successful people? Conversely, complainers seem to hang about with other complainers? We tend to surround ourselves with those who are similar to us.

Let's specifically discuss your interaction with negative individuals:

There will be those, struggling in their own lives, who carry the mindset that life happens TO them as opposed to the idea that they CREATE the life they are experiencing. They may also have these mindsets:

'everything just happens to me and I have no control over it'

'life is so hard, it's one long struggle'

'some people are lucky in life, and I'm not one of them'

'the world is a horrible place'

'men are jerks'

'women are crazy'

'people always have a hidden agenda, you can't trust anyone'

Some people make generalizations about the world based on a single personal experience. Do you have people in your life with this kind of mindset? Whether you are conscious of it or not, they will suck you down into their negativity, their sense of failure, or self-pity.

Have you ever heard the saying, "Misery loves company"? Well, it is quite true! The universal law of attraction affirms that like attracts like.

I've experienced this myself in work settings. Let me give you a personal example:

I was working at a job that I absolutely loathed. Morning after morning I would drag myself into the office, sit down at my desk and immediately look at the clock, counting the hours until lunch time. After lunch, I would do the same—counting the hours until it was time to leave. I was completely miserable.

I wasn't interested in the work I was doing. I was frustrated with the suppression of innovative ideas and at the lack of resources, I didn't like the way upper management treated the staff and didn't care for their strict rules: no coffee breaks, no food or drink at your desk and no talking to other employees. It felt more like a prison than a workplace.

I was not focused on gratitude, on the opportunity to make money or on creating a job that I loved. I was centered on every single little thing that I hated about my job.

I complained constantly to my friends at work and they did the same…. we complained to each other day in and day out, week after week, month after month. Some days we cried in the bathroom or in our cars, some days we sat angrily at our desks.

We had venting sessions during our lunch breaks, and even communicated after work hours to complain some more. I was pulling them into my pity party and they were recruiting me. We were 'feeding' each other consistently.

Because we agreed, we justified each other's complaining and I grew further and further entrenched in my scenario. I began to tell it to my family members and my friends outside of work. I would tell it to anyone who would listen! The more I told my 'I hate my job' story, the better I became at telling it. It became my identity.

It became my victim mentality. I was no longer a smart, educated, ambitious woman with imagination who loved to create new opportunities, brainstorm and collaborate. I was a mistreated, disrespected, undervalued, dispensable little worker bee who had no voice and merely went through the motions.

One day I sat at my desk and looked around the room—nothing had changed and nothing was going to change. I realized that complaining hadn't solved my problem. I was still right there, still feeling like a victim. Complaining was addictive, it temporarily made me feel good because I had empathy, support, and camaraderie from others. However, these 'good feelings' were treating the symptoms and not the cause. I was the cause. I needed to change myself—I needed to change my way of thinking.

I began to focus on positivity and growth. Once I reclaimed my identity as a smart, educated and ambitious person, I began reaching out to others who I saw as kind, smart, and successful. I wanted to leave the world of complaining, and join the world of positivity, service, and opportunities.
I started networking with successful people, reading all I could about them, researching, listening, communicating and surrounding myself with their positive energy. I threw out the victim mentality and replaced it with the drive to get things done!

You can change your thoughts this very moment...you always have control.

Protect your mindset ~your thoughts are an extremely powerful force. Positive or negative, results will follow your focus. What you focus on is what you create.

Knowing this will help you recognize those who are trying to bring you into their scenario. Those who have not achieved their career goals or have consistency struggled to maintain a successful relationship will often try to pull you into their negative belief system.

They want you to agree with them that 'it's just so hard', or 'there aren't any good candidates out there'.

What you focus on will result. You are communicating to your subconscious. Your subconscious (and the universe) work to fulfill your request.

If your emphasis is on the love and joy of finding the right one for you, you will find him or her. If your emphasis is on how 'difficult' it is to find the right one for you, then you will continue to experience 'difficulties'. Shifting your mindset will shift your life….one way or the other.

"Whether you think you can, or you think you can't—you're right."
— Henry Ford

Ward off energy vampires

When starting a conversation with a stranger, I tend to believe that they are friendly and authentic. I give everyone the benefit of the doubt. However, there are times when, in talking with someone, it hits me! I have been targeted!

Over the years, it has become easier for me to recognize these types of people early on in a conversation, but if you have trouble with this, pay close attention:

Many people call these 'energy vampires' because they do suck all the energy out of you. They usually have one or both of these motives:

1. They intend to USE you for your information, favors, expertise, connections, talents, position, advice, money or power to gain an advantage WITHOUT offering you anything in return. They have no respect or appreciation for

your time and energy.

2. They want to boost their confidence by bragging about themselves or their accomplishments (often known as fishing for compliments). They need someone (anyone) to be their audience.

Know how to quickly recognize these types of people and stop them in their tracks before they waste any more of your time and energy. Some sure signs of an energy vampire are:

1. They talk about themselves, their accomplishments and 'what they do' without letting you get a word in.

2. When you speak, they aren't truly listening to you, they're rehearsing what they are going to say next. They are simply waiting for you to stop talking so they can begin again.

3. When you speak, they talk over you, constantly interrupting you.

4. When the conversation drifts away from them and their talents/success/expertise, they either shift the discussion back to themselves or exit the conversation. They're not interested in talking to you or getting to know you.

5. The conversation is ALL about them.

6. If they do ask questions about you, their true motive is: determining if associating with you will benefit them.

7. They ask for favors but are conveniently unavailable when the time comes to do any for you.

There is an immense difference between an energy vampire and a person who asks for your help because they are genuinely in need.

Recently an old classmate of mine reached out to ask for my

knowledge and advice concerning a career change he was pursuing. He was extremely respectful of my time, explained his goals, asked a lot of questions, listened intently to my answers and thanked me for my time and energy. I was happy to speak with him and help him.

What a difference between this experience and one with an energy vampire!

Your time is precious. Stop wasting it with energy vampires. If one is preying on you, stop all contact and move on. Politely tell them you are not interested and cease communication.

If you're stuck in a work environment with one, simply excuse yourself to tend to an important task. After all, you are at work!

Quite often I have allowed energy vampires to waste my time and steal my energy. I tell you from personal experience that it is the most amazing feeling to stop them in their tracks and go on with your day.

The best part? You won't believe how much extra free time you'll have once you remove them from your space...as if your calendar completely opened up!

If you have ever said, "There is just not enough time in the day", or "If I only had more time I could enjoy _____", this is an excellent way to give yourself more time!

When in doubt, trust your gut instinct. If you feel uneasy around someone, ask yourself why. If you just have that funny feeling when meeting someone, take a moment to listen to your intuition. Don't shrug it off—pay attention.

Commit to yourself

I hope that by now you are beginning to see how important self-love is. I hope you are increasing your confidence and rediscovering all the wonderful things that make you uniquely you!

My hope for you is that you will utilize these transformation strategies to build the life you want. Implement them into your life immediately! Once you begin applying these strategies, you'll find yourself in the right mindset and energy to attract your desired outcome.

Let's put things into action! Make a commitment to yourself in writing:

I, _____, promise to practice self-love daily. I will nurture my self-confidence through positive and loving thoughts, behaviors, and actions, so that I can achieve my goals and create the life that I desire.

By writing this pledge, by putting pen to paper, you are solidifying the promise to yourself. It will become engraved in your subconscious and grow to be beyond powerful.

Knowing where and with whom to spend your time and energy

Have you heard the saying, "You have to kiss a lot of frogs before you find prince charming"? Rarely does anyone find their life partner on the first try. Rarely does the successful entrepreneur make it big on their first business idea. Rarely do you find your fulfilling career straight out of high school. It usually takes some trial and error until you create success for yourself.

You might be tired of kissing frogs, spending money, and consider giving up or you may be overwhelmed and feel that it simply takes too much time and effort to get where you want to be. If you are feeling discouraged, please remember something we discussed earlier—the WHY factor.

You can focus your energies on the right people, opportunities and investments by learning how to qualify and disqualify potential opportunities. Your qualifying skills are sharpened by listening to your intuition and enhancing your abilities for observing, listening, and processing information.

When you meet an opportunity, how do you size it up? How do you know if this opportunity will lead you towards what you want? Sharpening your observation skills will help you red flag those that are a waste of time and energy and become aware of the ones that will bring you closer to your goal.

Let's take relationships for example. Let's say you're searching for a business partner, a new client, a romantic partner or a new friend. When first talking with someone, you naturally share information about yourselves and you ask questions, prompting the other to share their own information and ideas ~this is the way a healthy conversation goes. When someone says, "Tell me about yourself", they're essentially saying *tell me why I should be interested in you/what's special about you?*

"Tell me about yourself" is an extremely open-ended request. One can say literally ANYTHING about themselves, so I listen attentively to the very first things they tell me. I gain insight into what they value most ~ which tells me a great deal about their self-image.

How listening carefully can save you

When it is their time to share, shut up and LISTEN! I mean REALLY listen. Listen with your ears, eyes, and your gut.

Observe their choice of words—you may hear expressions they use frequently and discover the meaning they associate with those words. Listen to their tone of voice.

Observe their body language, facial expressions, and their presence. What is it telling you?

Get a feel for their energy. If something seems 'off', listen to your intuition and ask yourself why you are feeling this way.

Gather information. Don't be quick to blurt out all about YOU. Being quiet is often your ally. You can't learn if you're talking.

Don't feel you must constantly fill the silence with unnecessary words. Let the stillness be there. Some people feel uncomfortable with quietness …. instead of jumping in with small talk, use this time to get a feel for their energy and body language.

Gather more information. If you feel the need to do something, a simple smile will do.

Often in life people don't feel 'heard', much less understood. Be the one who sincerely listens to this person and shows an interest in what they have to say. It is a kind thing to do, for which they will not only appreciate you, they will like you. (Note: your interest must be genuine and come from a place of authenticity, otherwise it will be recognized as insincere and have a negative effect on the conversation.)

Honoring your needs

Sometimes we become so focused on gaining the interest of the other person, that we forget to do some qualifying for ourselves. Remember, you are showing the other person how great it would be to be your partner, colleague, friend etc and they should be doing the same!

People who consistently neglect to qualify may have an underlying belief that they are 'not good enough', or that their needs are not important. If this sounds like you, the following example may be helpful:

I met with a lady who was actively searching for a long-term partner and had been on a few dates. When I asked her how the last date went, she began talking about whether she felt that the man liked her and was interested in seeing her again.

I let her talk, patiently waiting to hear her opinion of him. It never came. She said that he had asked to see her again so she thought the date had gone well.

I asked her if *she* wanted to see *him* again... did this man have the qualities and characteristics that she was looking for? She paused and stumbled over some 'ums' and 'I don't knows' and it was quickly apparent to me that she hadn't been thinking about what *she* truly wanted.

This woman was so accustomed to fulfilling a man's list of ideals and desires that she forgot to qualify him! She hadn't considered whether this man was worthy of her time and her attention!!

We went back to her list of qualities she was seeking in a romantic partner and I asked her if she had sensed any of these qualities in him. She replied yes to many of them, but there were a few she was unsure about. She went on another date with him, resolved to learn more about this man.

Let it serve as a reminder to you that your needs matter and that you maintain standards for your relationships.

8 STRATEGY #6 POSITION YOURSELF FOR OPPORTUNITY

'Where do I meet people?' is a common question among those looking to find their romantic partner, new friends, clients, mentors, etc. At the risk of sounding obvious, you must expand your opportunities. This is where ACTION comes into play. If you sit around your house waiting for Mr. or Mrs. Right to stop by, your prospects are very limited!

During a coaching session, I spoke with a highly successful career woman. She was extremely skilled at closing high end sales. She had no confidence issues when it came to business deals.

She was frustrated that she couldn't find the right man for her. She had been dating 'bad boys' who she would never consider marrying. We discussed where she was in her life, what her priorities were.

I asked her to day dream for a minute, and to picture her ideal man. She began to describe a handsome, strong, silent type. He was sexy in an 'I'm comfortable in my own skin' way. He was dressed in a sophisticated manner. He was not flashy, not begging for attention.

An intelligent man, he could hold a serious and articulate conversation. He was experienced and talented in his career. He was strong, but also kind and caring. She described a man who would be a 'rock' for her and her future family. She was extremely frustrated that she hadn't found someone who matched this description!

I asked her what she did for fun socially. She said that she didn't get out much because she had just moved to a new city and only knew people from work. Aha! "Well, you certainly can't meet the man of your dreams if you never leave your home," I told her. She agreed. We discussed various ways she could increase the probability of meeting her dream man. There were local organizations that interested her, yet she was tentative about joining and attending social events. This is where we began.

Often it is fear that prevents us from meeting new people. We are afraid of the unknown ~ afraid to go somewhere new, afraid we will feel awkward and embarrassed because we don't know anyone there.

The surest way to meet new people at an event is to show up alone. If you go with a friend, you often end up talking only to your friend, you feel tethered to them, you may be afraid to leave your comfort zone. When you show up alone, you may already be out of your comfort zone, but you will soon discover you are open and free to talk to anyone and you can easily float from one conversation to another.

Learn from the past but be focused in the present

If you have made mistakes in the past, good! It means you have fallen on your face and experienced failure. Contrary to popular belief, failure is a good thing.

What?

Yes, I said it ~ failure is a good thing ~ it is our greatest teacher. If you have experienced heartache, frustration, anger, or sadness from a negative situation in the past, you know very deeply how that feels. You have a vivid picture of what that life involves. This is your motivation to never allow that to happen again.

Your past experiences teach you what you want and what you

don't want. They can also teach you something about what type of person you were in that time frame. Of course, roles can change depending on the dynamic of the people involved, but often it's a fantastic learning experience to make changes as needed.

Perhaps there are some things that you hope to change. Maybe you would like to work on yourself, on your own personal growth and development, on being the person you wish to be. Perhaps you want to be more affectionate, more independent, more patient, speak kinder words, set healthier boundaries...

Our past experiences can provide us with insights as to what we want to change—about ourselves and about our outlook on life. As our views change, we grow wiser in choosing the people we spend time with. Our sense of intuition grows stronger.

Learning from the past is essential to growth and to improving our lives but dwelling on the past means you risk missing out on the present and the future.

Here is a simple guideline:

1. Realize the issue or mistake

2. Ask: Why did this not work for me

3. Ask: What can I do to avoid this or overcome this obstacle in the future

4. Learn the lesson and store it in your knowledge bank for later use

Those who dwell on the past become stuck in their old mindsets, stuck in their lives—unable to make the forward progress needed to enjoy new and fulfilling experiences.

I coached a beautiful, intelligent lady who was independent and made avid practice of self-love. She was divorced, had had some relationships since then, but was really looking for her long-term companion ~ someone with whom she could share the rest of her life.

She was attracting men who were emotionally unavailable or did not want to commit to her.

During our coaching sessions, I found that she would often get sidetracked by bringing up wounds from the past. Clearly her focus was not in the present and not on her goal of finding a long-term companion. She was primarily focused on what had happened in her previous relationships and in her former marriage.

What your focus is…what you pour your energy into, will bring about results in your life.

If you are focused on generating new clients, you will behave and act in ways that bring you into conversation with many people, and you will build your business.

If you are focused on exercising three times a week, you will act in ways that keep you active and your health will improve.

If you are focused on what went wrong in the past, you will act from the mindset you were in when those things happened and you will again attract the same results.

How can you truly move forward if you are looking backwards?

How much faster you will get there if your head is forward and your gaze is focused on the target!

Try this silly exercise and see for yourself! Go outside and pick a target far away. Try to run towards that target while turning your head and looking behind you. See how awkward is it to run this way? Your balance is off and your body is out of alignment. Because your eyes are not fixed on the target you cannot see to avoid the obstacles that are in your way.

Now run with your head facing forward and eyes on the target. You are balanced and running much faster. You can see clearly in front of you and are able to adjust to any obstacles that are in your way.

Dwelling on past failures holds no purpose for you. Learn from them, store the lesson in your knowledge bank and don't look back. Focus on the present. Once my client realized she was dwelling on the past, she began to correct this. She shifted her focus to the present and she was open to attracting the man and relationship that she wanted. Her ability to see others clearly and use her intuition became greater because her focus was on the here and now. Her judgement was no longer clouded by the past.

She began to disqualify men who did not have the attributes she wanted in a partner and became stronger in setting standards for herself—not settling as she had in the past. It was wonderful to see this change in her! She would no longer make the same mistakes by settling for those who would not reciprocate her love and effort.

Being present will open you up to opportunities and allow you to recognize them so you can act upon them. Remember, if you never go anywhere new or try anything different, your life will stay the same. If you simply think positive thoughts and repeat mantras to yourself without taking action, you will not see the results you wish to see. If you sit around and think, but don't *do,* you become the philosopher, not the innovator, hero, leader, or great adventurer.

Thought—Behavior—Action—Result

New thoughts transition into new behaviors, and when you take new actions, you will produce new results. If you don't like the way things are in your life, if you haven't achieved the results you want, start at the beginning with a new positive thought based in reality and transition through the sequence until you produce what you desire.

Use the strategies I have shared with you to tap into your personal power and make the changes you seek. It won't happen overnight—Rome wasn't built in a day! But as you take the first step forward, you begin your journey towards a better you and a better life. It may not be perfect at first. You may feel uncomfortable, make a mistake, or feel as if things aren't happening fast enough—but have patience with yourself. Give yourself time. Invest in yourself. You're worth it!

9 YOUR LEGACY

If you find yourself slipping into your old mindset patterns, acknowledge the fact, work to remove them immediately, and keep moving forward. None of us are perfect and we will encounter obstacles and problems along life's journey. We have all made mistakes. The key is to learn from them: use these lessons to grow, to move forward, to create better relationships and fuller lives.

One day I decided that my life was going to change.

Once I made that decision, I began to change my mindset, build my confidence, and take the steps necessary for me to move forward.

Believe in yourself and believe in your own personal power to make a real change.

It all begins with a decision—a choice you make that things WILL change. By implementing the strategies in this book, you create shifts in your mindset ~ which create shifts in your behaviors and actions ~ which create the results you want in your life. The sooner you create these shifts, the sooner you will see results! It has been my pleasure to guide you along this journey to claiming your personal power. If you find yourself needing additional coaching and support, please visit www.janacorinne.com for information and coaching opportunities.

I hope this book has helped bring awareness and clarity to you. I hope this book has helped to ignite that spark within you. If you want to lead an authentic life, I cannot stress strongly enough the importance of first developing your self-thinking, then behaving and taking action towards BEING the person that you want to be. When you live authentically, fulfilling your own basic needs first, you will create the relationships you desire, the career or business that you want and share your beautiful gifts with others.

Ultimately, your inner light will shine brightly and warm all those around you ~ your legacy will reach far and wide.

Now let's see what you can do!

ABOUT THE AUTHOR

Jana Corinne is a certified strategic intervention life coach, entrepreneur consultant, and author of the new book "The Confident You". Pulling from her coaching and consulting practice, Jana shares the strategies from her own life transformations and those of her clients. Jana has an MBA from Florida Gulf Coast University and a certification from the Robbins-Madanes Center for Strategic Intervention. Jana lives in Central Kentucky with her husband, daughter, and loyal pup Winston. She spends each spring wearing derby fascinators while sipping mint juleps. Visit www.janacorinne.com for more about Jana.

61144216R00050

Made in the USA
Columbia, SC
20 June 2019